To

Phoebe

Keep on Inspiring the
World.

x

[signature]

STREETS

The Profit & The Poet

Foreword

As a child, I experienced the breakdown of family and all it brings with it, never once given an opportunity to express how I was feeling. My voice was unheard, forgotten if you will, and there was not a platform to share my own experiences. As an adult, I have experienced first-hand the impacts of heartache and heartbreak, family breakdown and upheaval. As a mother, I have often felt like I am fighting a never-ending battle to establish routine with child contact. It is difficult and sometimes frustrating, as I am sure many single mothers will tell you, but I persevere regardless, grateful that the father of my children wants to be present in their lives. While I could write for days and tell you about my own experiences, reading this book gave me time to think about the other side of the spectrum. The perspective of a father who wants to see his children, of a male broken heart, a mind overwhelmed with reminiscence and regret, is one I have yet to explore myself.

He claims to be a preacher of the streets, but does Streetz Preacher live up to his name? I believe so. At Socktober Fest, a charitable event in October 2014, I had the pleasure of hearing him share his experience and passion for supporting homeless people. He shared his own story, a dedicated advocate for implementing social change, the front man of Give Back Brum. Though I do not know him well, the reputation attached to his name goes before him. He denounces all labels assigned to him by society, explores aspects of mental health, contradictions and stereotypes. His no-nonsense approach in addressing social injustice had me intrigued about the contents of this book. It did not disappoint.

In my own writing, I examine family relationships, the implications of family breakdowns, mostly focusing on mother-daughter relationships and the issues they face. In essence, I write what I know.

The Profit & The Poet

I write what I understand to be my truth in its rawest form. I believe a great writer shares an element of themselves in their work, making it unique and sincere. As a reader, I like to be able to relate, to apply the written words to an aspect of my own life or those around me, feeling as though the writer has taken a step into my life or introduced me to theirs. Reading this book gave me an insight to a point of view I had not considered before now. It gave alternative views and opinions on situations that I frequent often. You may have heard that there are two sides to a story and this book reflected that and more.

At the heart of this book, is a man who is conscious about the lessons his children will learn from him, in all areas of life. He speaks, writes and lives his truth unapologetically. The book itself is a representative of voices at the frontline of society. While it does not exist to speak for you, may it speak to you in ways that open up the confines of a closed mind and helps you to consider that alternative point of view.

It is my absolute pleasure to introduce to you, Profit & Poet by Streetz Preacher.

Annika Spalding
Author of Shattered Dreams, The Soaring Butterfly and Reflections.

The Profit & The Poet

A Message from Juice

"I met Andy before I met the StreetzPreacher. A tall racist football hooligan looking guy with a calm doorman about to do damage demeanour. Then I found out he was not only a man of faith but a father of Black, mixed-race children.

His measured words were his bond, whether speaking on his helping to combat homelessness or his research into mental health issues and work with at risk people.

At every turn his poems would pop up on social media with a bunch of friends saying how much of a help his words were to them. Having seen him at work with those in need it all made sense to me. This was the perfect guy to speak on these issues as he has been through so many of them. And here he was, still standing tall, calm and measured as ever.

Whatever you think of these words know this: these words come from a very real place and have proven ability to bring that same towering calm to the most frustrated and lonely of minds. A Preacher for the Streetz."

Juice Aleem (2014)

The Profit & The Poet

Growing up in a neighbourhood just outside of the grandeur of Bournville with its chocolate smelling air and its big green open spaces, it was hard to see poverty. Yes, there were poor people, holes in socks, bad odours, scuffed shoes, un-brushed teeth, grease laden hair and ill-fitting coats covering peoples' cigarette imbrued cable knit cardigans. But that's about as bad as we had it. Yes, we had the local vagabond or tramp as we used to call him, but he was the local drunk who lived out of a baby pram with one bad misshaped wheel. Everyone knew him as Arthur.

No one knew his story, well at least no one I know did, we all guessed about why he was homeless, if he indeed wasn't fooling all of us and lived in a mansion. Yet one summer I went with my friends to the local factory centre, basically a newly developing business park close to where we lived, we played army and tracking in the disused area at the side of the building site. One day I went to our den; three pallets and some branches over the top of it in reality, and in there was Arthur. The man of few words, unkempt beard and awful smell, was now living in our five-star base. He was asleep and I left him that way.

 Now fast forward to today, after being homeless myself and having very little support to get back on my feet, I have a clearer understanding of why people like Arthur are stereotyped as having very little to say, is it because they are ignorant and don't want to be disturbed. Or is it the fact that nobody tries to understand and take the time to enter their world and really have a conversation with them. We all make decisions in life that affect where our journey takes us, for some its fighting with their parents, for others it's years of abuse in a relationship without knowing how to get out until it's too late, for some it is a simple lifestyle choice.

These choices are in all of our lives, yet we often take for granted that from the outside looking in we can judge who is doing well in life and who is struggling, yet how often do we step in to those lives uninvited and try to impose our morals on those who we think we can help? Rather than just making conversation and be invited in? In my 5 years of working in a community of which I was also a resident for almost a year on the streets and in a car, it is astounding to see how many people think they know best, the guy outside the supermarket asking for change must surely need another sandwich, so we ignore the carrier bag of food next to him and go and spend £5 on a meal deal instead. Completely self-absorbed with what we believe he needs in order to satisfy our own judgement of his situation.

It is not just the ordinary members of the public that make this mistake of overlooking the real problems for the rough sleepers in our country. It is the multi million pound charities that profess to work with the otherwise socially excluded and yet cannot tell you where those "service users" are sleeping tonight, they throw resources at the stereotypical media enforced issues, rather than seeking to build relationships with those very same individuals they call users.

Not many people actually treat that individual as a human, they just try to treat the symptoms or the virus sleeping rough. The misconception that if someone asks for money they must be wanting it for alcohol or drugs is mythical. Most drug users will tell you they need drug money. Most alcoholics will tell you they need a drink because they are "rattling". There is a huge misconception that beggars can't be choosers. If that's the case why is that not applied when people say they chose this lifestyle? It is this wishy washy approach and judgement to the stereotype applied to rough sleepers as a community that was also applied to other "minority" communities throughout history and we all know the repercussions of marginalising people for our own gain, financially and societally.

It is for these reasons that I have written this book, to give more incite in to what we lack as a society in both empathy and the giving of ourselves and our time to the plight and needs of others, in such a way that it is they who benefit and not just to make ourselves feel adequate because we tried to recreate a YouTube video scenario of fake giving back.

In Birmingham, UK, we had our very own Brum Spiderman, he was an internet sensation for about eighteen hours, he dressed up and fed homeless people for one day, he was then seen wherever the television cameras were, for a further week. He was given exposure as doing something great for others, yet he isn't out here today. And hasn't been seen for over a year by the regular; less public volunteer services in the city. It is this bandwagon marketing of do-gooder's that creates more of a problem for the community, as it makes them targets for others to make a name for themselves at the expense of exposing people who are sometimes sleeping on the streets away from the eyes of the world, because they are running away or hiding from people who are really trying to harm them.

Without knowing their stories, these vulnerable humans are being thrust in to the spotlight without knowing or realising the consequences to themselves, hence the reason why they are vulnerable in the first place. We as society must not only take responsibility, we must also take some of the blame too. If we take the blame and make it our problem, we can then become the solution. And the key to learning is listening and challenging. Listen to what the rough sleepers are telling us and challenge the perception that society and media instils on us. Break the stereotype and then give back in the right way. Then and only then will we stop the exploitation of the community and unite against poverty on this level.

Andrew Pittaway, Author.

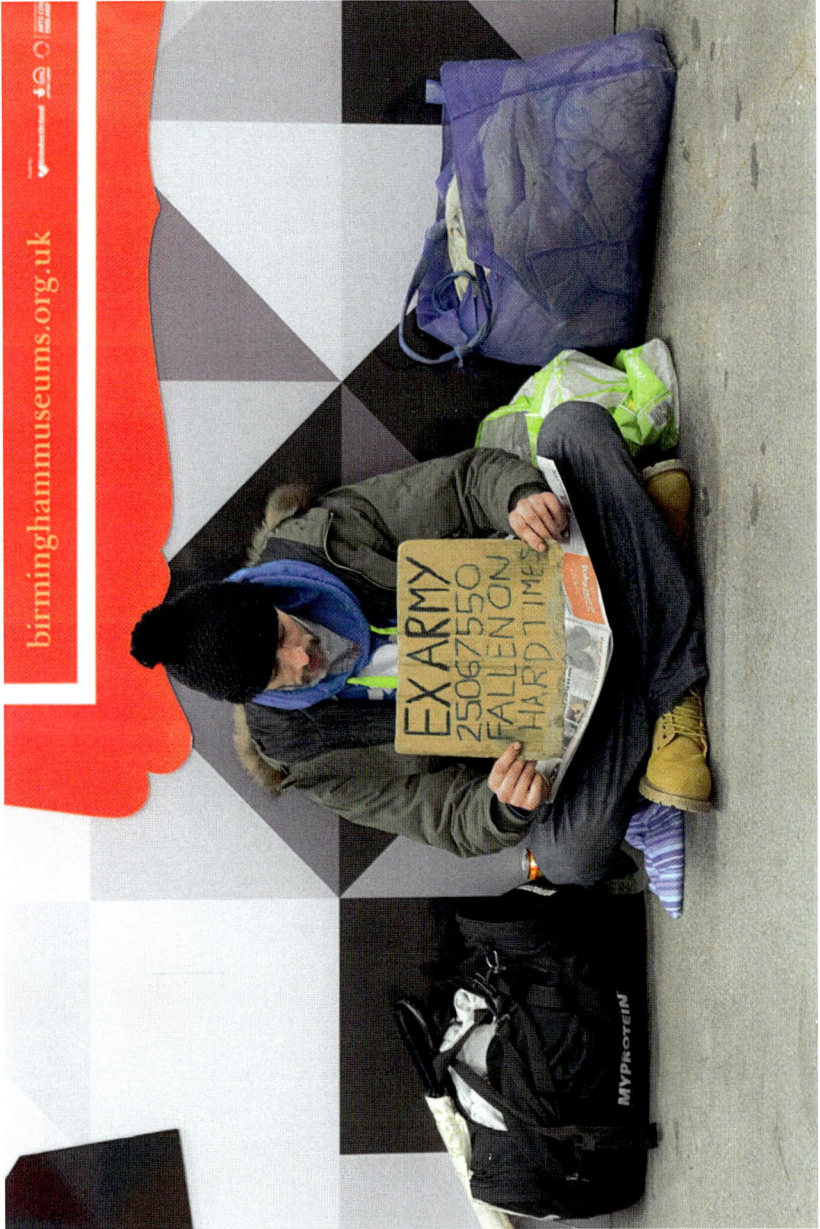

The Profit & The Poet

<u>Mess</u>

How did I get into this mess?
Looking back on my life,
I'm realising there's nothing left,
Realising all that fantasising about greatness,
Just ending up being stress,
Lusting for more, when now I've ended up with even less,
These pavements are home for the very near future,
This is just my story,
Maybe you can read my future,
Maybe you can take something out of my life,
I already took out my home, my kids, my wife,
Now they're somebody else's
They give him my pleasure,
When you're as low as me,
Conversation is treasure
Just being listened to is enough food for my soul,
Look into my eyes,
Do you see how we roll?
The life of a vagrant.

The Profit & The Poet

<u>The temptation of Cider</u>

I wasn't always alcoholic,
But since I've been outside I've become dependent on it,
Sort of like hypochondriacs addicted to paracetamol,
Just a quick fix that you can become reliant on,
You may judge me and say this is the reason I'm homeless,
But the truth is,
I'm treated like a dog anyway,
And now cider is my owner,
Self-medicated I'm on nothing harder,
Than the floor I'm calling my bed,
This nectar takes away the loss of my father,
You see we all have tragedies,
A story to share,
But it's so hard to be heard always sitting down here.
If I didn't have cider
I'd always be sober
And then those heartbreaking thoughts of everything I had,
Will be as hurtful as when sometimes,
I've had too much and the 3 litre spills over,
I don't know where I'm heading, but I know where I've been,
Don't call me alcoholic,
Because this deep rooted pain of losing everything,
Is why I hide away from the public?
The shame of not wanting to be seen

The Profit & The Poet

The Start

A simple text (why dads struggle to remain civil to their ex)

"You can't have them this week
End of text."

Then you wander why we can't talk without me getting vexed?
Who made you their only parent?
And put me in a position in their eyes,
So somehow they don't care...
Who are you to dictate to me when I can see my children,
Who are half of me,
Telling me I have to pay the price for our relationship collapse,
When I'm paying every day they aren't with me,
consider this perhaps,
Who bought them into this world with you,
Who was holding your hand?
When the midwife let our daughters' head rip you,
As you pushed too hard then; now I'm tearing,
I can't look you straight in the eye without cursing and swearing,
Paint me out to be uncaring,
But I'm paying the price for my broken heart you force me to keep wearing,
I know it's a game to you,
Its control,
But you report my behaviour to the police, get me locked up for 16 hours, with
no charges I add,
While you sleep with a stranger and call me the unstable parent in court,

With no proof to back up your false allegations,
and your solicitor grinning like she's already won in this for you.
How many Saturdays did I turn up early, just to be told you'll have to stand at
the end of the drive and wait,
But the one day I call you and say I'm stuck in traffic,

I apologize profusely,
but you tell me you're not having them today

The Profit & The Poet

You're late.

I just ask one thing without getting angry,
if you love your child why do you do this,
because at the end of the day yeah I'm suffering,
But my children should never have to go through this,

Making me pay up front like I'm renting my kids,
Then go telling tales about how I didn't give you enough when I lost my job
but you still wanted 350 a month payments,
To go spend on your new drive way or other house modifications you did.
But it's my children who are hurting,
I call; you tell them to hang up, they have to ask permission to even answer
the phone because they are not certain,
If they are allowed to answer freely,
can't use face time,
because you're worried they'll see me,
and they want to come see me at my house,
stay over and enjoy their time with daddy,
that weakens your control over them so you make sure they can't hear me..

All this from just a simple text.

Then you wander why we can't talk as adults without me getting vexed...

The Profit & The Poet

<u>Side Piece</u>

I'm some bodies morning and I'm some bodies night,
The life of a side piece there's no substance,
In between times,
how I'm living isn't right,
Don't want to commit because I've been through all that,
Got the kids to prove it,
I am not going to go back,
So instead I'll be used and make them feel used too...
Because with no commitment there's no love,
And it's easier to do,
But what sort of a person am I to raise my kids and say I love you,
When my actions are telling them I'm confused, and I honestly am probably
confusing you too,
I'm showing them that they don't need a lifelong soul to intertwine with,
as long as I've got some body,
To have sex and to dine with,
It doesn't matter if they meet somebody they would love to spend time with,
Because when my children use me as their first role model,
That they just let out a big sigh with,
disappointed disjointed life planned out before them,
I better find love soon Because this guilty life I'm living is not one to applaud
when,
I can't show my children this is what life is about,
having nothing to call your own and without deposits of love,
There's nothing left to draw out,
No love is not a transaction it's so much more than that,
But remaining a side piece I'm only reinforcing that I only expect my kids to
live up to that.

So I'm cutting everyone off,
No midnight flirty talking,
I promise myself this, 'til my eyes fall on the next fit one to walk in

The Profit & The Poet

You see loneliness is like an addiction,
I need to get help from this mental affliction,
Find comfort in someone and start to settle down,
because my children are suffering with each new one I bring around.

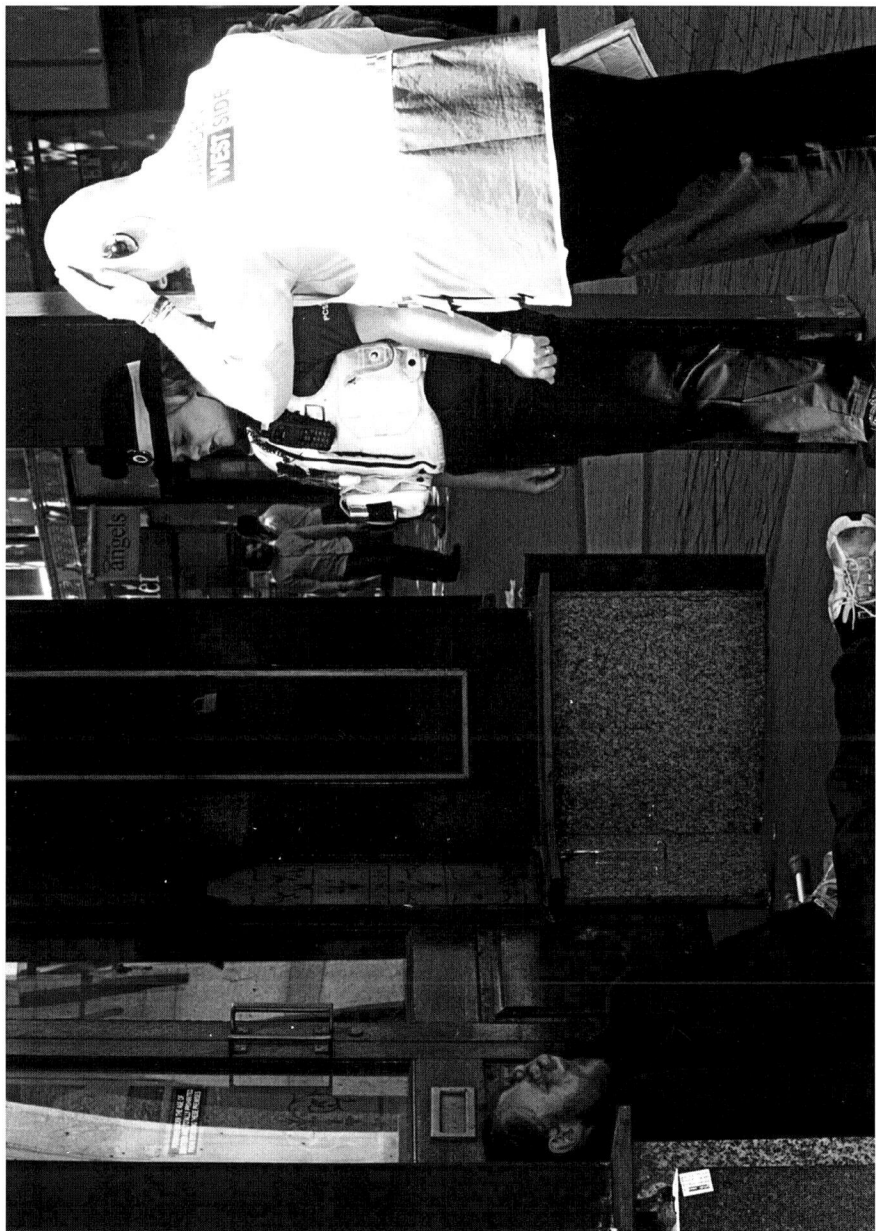

The Profit & The Poet

Soul'd out: a poetic journey...

I'm going after those that came after me...
If you do not understand metaphors
Then don't come after me
You cannot and will not remotely understand
Because you uphold your personal opinion
Above the law of the land
Police officer you wicked overseer
Intimidate the weak but gun down the pioneer...
You'll never take me alive copper
So you try to kill me in a slow death
Sit on my chest and force my last breath
Then you get found not guilty of acting improper
Out of uniform you smile with your friends
But put on your costume
And the message that it sends
It never ends
Your barbaric behaviour
And your colleagues back you up
But when you caught on your own
A 17 year old kid can back you up
You operate with their agenda
But you should have never pushed this
Because where there's no beef
There's no peace
No justice
You are the criminal
You make the law up as you go
But when I ask you what the law is
It is funny you don't know
You try to get smart and when I ask you what your name is
You offer me your collar
Like a dog
That's how they got you trained

The Profit & The Poet

Bitch do you not see
That you sold out to the system
Everything they do is a reflection
Like the light refracting from the prism
You think you're free
But you're the one imprisoned
Because one day you'll have to stand against your boss
But then they'll pull out your file
And sit opposite you with a smile
While reading all your misconduct charges they conveniently lost
When complaints were made they had your back
But now you got to face it
Police don't want the "coloured " man
Because the system only profits
By being racist.

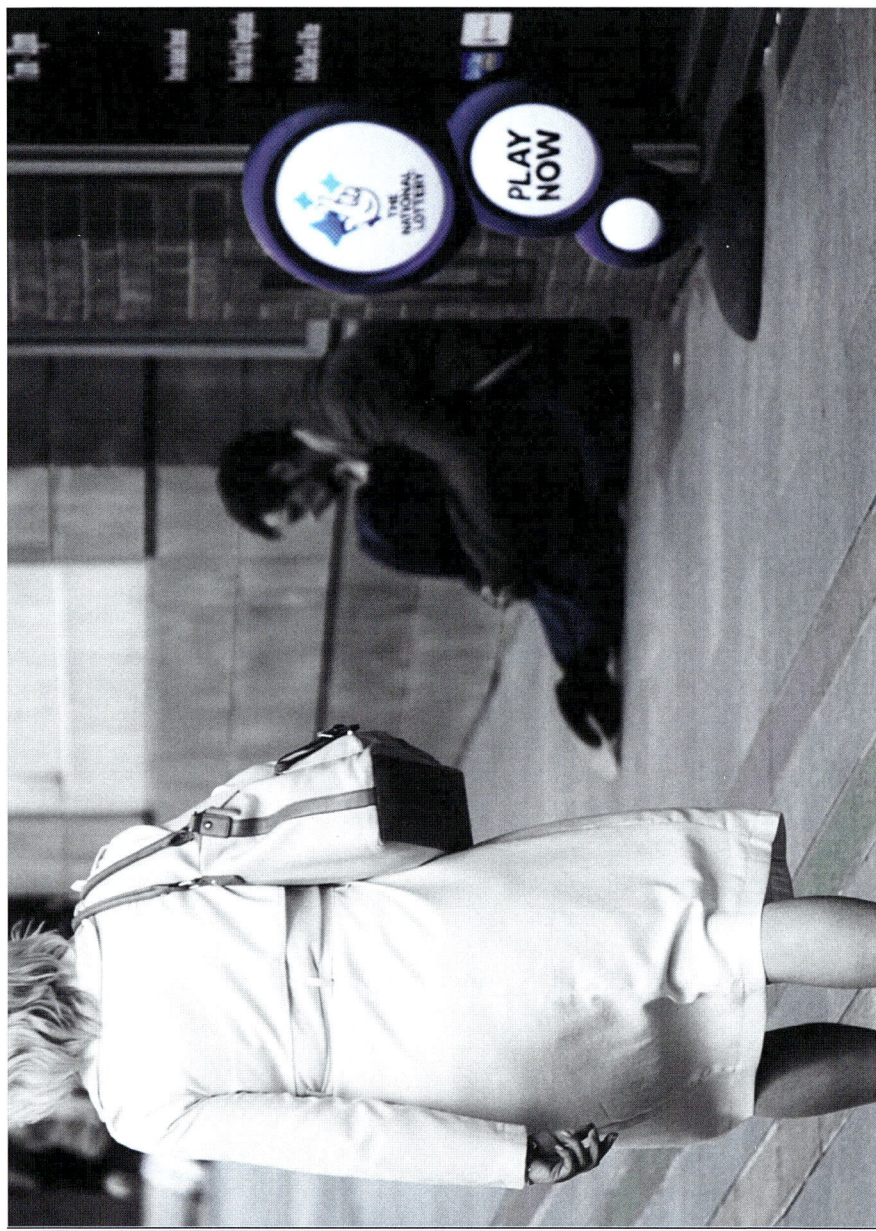

The Profit & The Poet

Slave Master

Let's get Black people to do our work for us,
Keep it moving,
So they die as poorers,
Di-as-poras,
Die as poor as we want them to suffer in,
Condition their kids mindset,
Keep them suffering,
Keep us up with them,...
Keep us up with him,
Who is he?
The white slave master,
European,
Your-hope-in,
This world,
That's all you can hope for,
A white Jesus,
Is who you put your Hope in,
Forgetting that he couldn't be white in Jeru - Shalem,
The City of the Hebrews,
Where the Moors stood strong to teach you,
Do not let "black history" be for one month,
It's your life time's work to educate other people,
Keep hope alive,
To quote Jesse,
Don't ever let the slave mentality
Oppress me,
Or oppress you,
We in this as brothers,
No secret society,
We blowing their covers,
Their cover ups,
Are no longer hidden,
We got access to the truth,

The Profit & The Poet

That was forbidden,
So let's keep spreading the truth,
Keep the mindsets focused of our youth,
Show them,
Let them show us,
Don't ever let your children say
" he never knew us"
Stay present,
That's your gift,
Show them the right and wrong ways how to live,
Don't let the white privilege man control you,
Don't let the white man's system just hold you,
We are no longer chained,
Break free from the shackles in your mind ,
And you will never be enslaved

The Profit & The Poet

Mind games

Do I not have the right to ask,
When I see the world tricking my mind into thinking I'm the one wearing that
mask,
All I get told is keep it real,
Yet I'm constantly fed lies by the guys who broadcast the news, airing their
thoughts for YouTube views,

What's the big deal?
Opening conscious conversation,
With a lexicon for correlation,
Way above my pay grade,
Offering it free without deprivation to those who are lost in this false
advertised world that was once beautifully and wonderfully made,

But I don't get angry or let my suicidal thoughts hang me,
out to dry like some hand me,
Down garms,
I just allow my mind to settle,
Like that unboiled kettle,
Out to blow up at the flick of a switch so then everyone can blame me for my
outburst and go up in arms,
Wrestling those thoughts,
As I share what's important,
Rather than post on the internet all the latest adverts that are gonna rot your
insides like those unlucky charms,

Battling chemical castration of the pineal gland,
calcifying the third eye,
And…
Then wandering why you're to blind to see,
But if you live of this world,
Valuing diamonds and pearls,
Undressing of valuing the person you should be,

The Profit & The Poet

What's the big deal?

You are gracing this earth like a king straight from birth,
But not in search of your crown,
You lust for theirs,
Then you will never have your own,
Want to act childish and live like a Man,
There's a conflict inside you,
Saying you don't need to be grown,

But spiritually blind,
With that calcified mind,
Your world starts to unravel as the rotation of the planet continues to travel,
Orbiting like Apollo 9,
Lost in space ,
Cannot reenter,
No going back into that placenta,

Your comfort zone no longer exists in that self-built womb you where thought
you were safe,
So if you are happy to stay in that limbo,
Not knowing the order in which things go,
You're just another lost profit for the government masters,
Banking on your failure in the human race.

The Stranger Walking Past

She was sun kissed naturally,
The complexion of a Goddess,
Hair wild like the branches of a youthful tree,
She holds herself humble and modest,

Feminine beauty,
Feminist attitude,
Advocating her sex,
Not disrespectful or rude,

Leading her movement,
Following her dream,
Making it happen,
On the creative scene,

Is she the person?
Who she needed to be,
Overcoming her worst fear,
And her anxiety,

Inspiration for her peers,
All over the world,
Amazing beauty,
Maturity of a woman,
Innocence of a girl.

The Profit & The Poet

<u>My</u>

Emotions are like oceans,
They crash,
They wave even if you don't wave back,
Turmoil got you spinning like a cyclone of frustrated imbalance,
Duality of a split personality hangs on your last chance,
Or is it their last chance,
Are they ready,
To sprinkle their love at last...
Like the showering feeling of freshly thrown confetti,
My emotional rollercoaster is high,
Because with the dips and the lows I am so slow that I close my eyes as I feel
the world just flash by,
So while I'm up here,
I'm taking in the view,
But I feel empty,
Like a house with no occupation,
I have no key,
I can't gain entry to my mind,
Because I don't have me.

The Profit & The Poet

<u>Poverty</u>

Born and raised inside or outside of a border,
Creates space and a place for the powerful to maintain order,

But the ordered are restricted by the box they are placed in,
Whether its faith or our race that they capitalise on wasting,

Our resources
Stolen to pay for military forces,
While the corridors of wall street,
Match the corridors of blood,
They honour the few that rise out of the hood,

Is it good enough that our voices are drowned out while they have their own channels,
Broadcasting war,
As they talk about peace on those panels,
Question time , but they never give answers,
Spend billions killing, while we all die from cancers,

They know there's a cure for all diseases including poverty,
But if there's no poor,
There's no reason to build property,
Look at it properly there's a system in place,

Included or excluded by the complexion of your face,
Or your accent or your state education,
Told to get degrees and doctorates,
But that's 3 or 4 years more programming which just leads to frustration,

If you don't see it then stop watching TV,
Because the messages they send you are like what's app,
They're free,
Free at a cost now there's a thought for the blind,

The Profit & The Poet

You still don't see that they cost you in spirit in mind,

Can't hear must feel then,
Is that how it is set,
Expecting to see truth on a box made to broadcast the agenda,

Flat screen,
And HD,
They tell us lies in 3D

They call it on demand,
But we didn't ask for any of this remember,

It's light entertainment well so was
Jim'll fix it,
They protected Rolf Harris,
but can you tell what it is yet?

Some of us can and some of us still don't get it,

They send us a card,
And then take all our credit,
We own the banks,
But still we are in debit,

This message is sponsored by truth...
Should I delete, or press

Send it...

The Profit & The Poet

Regrets

My heart is longing,
To belong in,
Your heart,
Your mind,
Your judgments wrong,
In years from now,
You'll see I'm right,
But you're blinded by this piercing light,
It is so bright,
It's made me dark,...
In that place you call your heart,

It's at these times,
I wish I could rewind time,
Show you the real me,
Open your eyes,
But that can't happen,
We're too far gone,
You sleep with him,
I sleep alone,
I can't call you,
Just in case he moans,
Regrets of the things we got wrong,
Now I don't know where to start...

Regrets

The Profit & The Poet

<u>Some things to think about</u>

If I said "I love you", how many would know what I mean? And who would believe me?

A word thrown like confetti at a wedding has no value after it's thrown,

Yet a word said from the heart, will always have value to another heart...

....
You cannot feed a closed mouth;
the same applies to a closed mind.
....

A pair of scissors doesn't have to be in perfect condition to cut, likewise a person doesn't have to be perfect to achieve their goal...

Your perception of yourself can either hold you back or push you forward toward your aim...

Think about it...

The Profit & The Poet

Why a woman needs to forgive and men need to be honest.

Jeff was 23 when he got with sally,
Sally was 18,
Sally had been in an abusive relationship and ended it just a month earlier,
Jeff had too. He had been stabbed and attacked by his ex,
Both vowed never to be that way with each other,

8 years later they realised that their pledge was a lie,
Sally had an affair, Jeff had issues he had never shared with anyone, not even
Sally.
They broke up and Jeff quickly entered into a new relationship with Anna, she
too had been in an abusive relationship,
Jeff promised not be like her ex, for almost a year their relationship was
perfect, then the lies crept in from both of them,
Jeff saw the signs and left,
Anna moved on with Matthew,

Jeff stayed single.

He bumped in to Sally, after 5 years she was single too,
They talked but they were never going to get back together, even though it
was love,
She couldn't forgive his lies at the beginning of their relationship, in front of
her stood a changed man, but she still saw the liar in him.
He saw the liar too, but he also had learned on his journey to tell the truth, he
left Anna and countless others because they were just like him,

Liars.

His time being single revealed that he would have to start telling the truth,
even about the smallest things,
The reason why he was late home, the reason he hadn't cooked,
the reason why he had no money, Yet Sally had not changed.

The Profit & The Poet

She still couldn't forgive, she still saw a liar in front of her,
she wasn't willing to admit she too had lied, and yet he never held it against
her. He just pointed out that she too was a liar like him.

He reflected on the fact that she went off with another man and was happy to
believe that guys' lies, and forgive them because they were lies he was telling
to his wife, not to her.
Yet a man she so clearly loved who was a liar, she held a grudge. And the man
she loved now had less than ever before. A sleeping bag and a mis-shaped
wooly hat, he still had his smile. She couldn't take that from him.

Note to all:

Be honest in everything you do.

Note to self:

If you can forgive a liar, he will one day start to trust you and tell you the
truth, no matter how harsh it is...

Jeff. Well Jeff was code for Andy. All other names have been changed. But
telling the truth will always breed trust. So I may as well be honest.

The Profit & The Poet

Escape

I'm gonna run, gonna run,
Til I run out of road,

Where I end up only God above knows,

I feel like Forrest Gump tryna run away from my past,

But its catching up with me,
Cuz my life story was fast,

Chorus:

Caught up in a whirlwind of love and of loss,
I gotta escape from this hurt, no matter the cost,
my story.

I hurt you so bad but I say I that still love you,

I go out with her and hold hands,
Have a dance,

But still say there's no one above you,

Chorus :

Caught up in a whirlwind of love and of loss,
I gotta escape from this hurt, no matter the cost,
my story.

I say I don't care who sees us as long as it's not you,
I left you at home with my babies,
Because I know that I've got you,
But while I was in bed with her,
That's when I went and forgot you,

The Profit & The Poet

Chorus:

Caught up in a whirlwind of love and of loss,
I gotta escape from this hurt; no matter the cost,
my story.

So I'm running but it feels like I'm going nowhere,
I can still smell your scent,
and feel you lying on my chest hair,
I got this hole in my heart and I don't care,
Because I'm running to you to say sorry,
Even if you don't wanna listen when I get there,

Chorus:

Caught up in a whirlwind of love and of loss,
I gotta escape from this hurt, no matter the cost,
Our story.

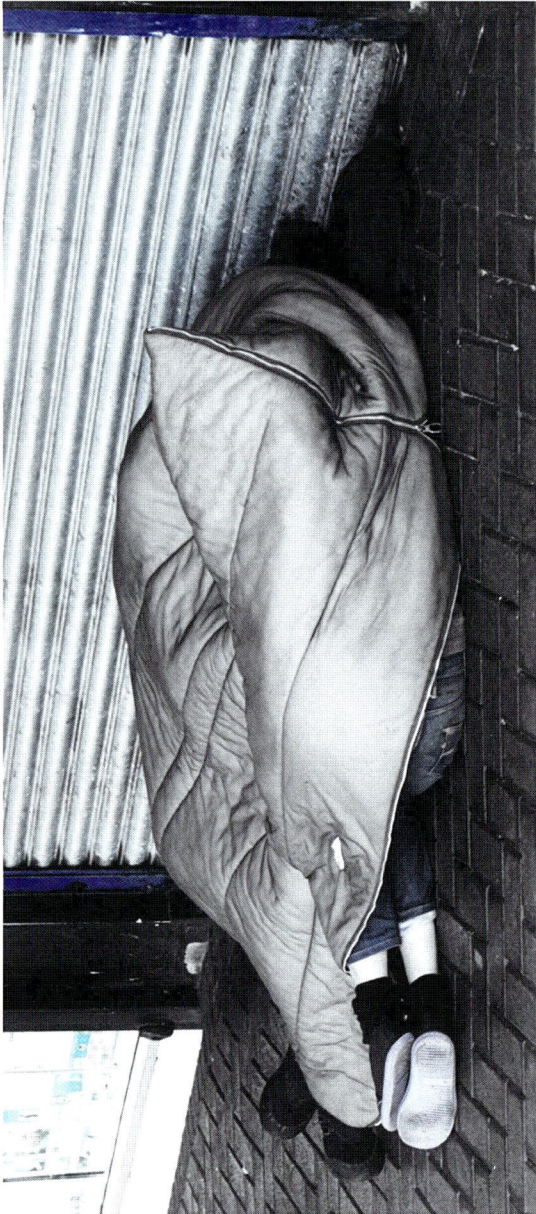

The Profit & The Poet

Love Concept

If I gave my life for you, you'd say I was your hero,
But if I gave my life for a stranger you'd probably say I'm foolish,

What makes you more important than a stranger if we are all the same,
Your selfish reasoning is no reason at all, it's just the way you're stained,

You're mind has been imbrued with these things to make you have self-lust,
You confuse this with loving yourself, because the ...selfish world says you
must,

It's not love to treat yourself better than a person you don't know,
It's love to sacrifice your own joy,
If it helps someone else truly glow,

But first you need to understand love and it seems most of you don't really
know it's real definition,
You personalise it to suit yourself ,
And that seems to be enough to perpetuate your fact that's really fiction,

The Profit & The Poet

<u>The Parent Trap</u>

When a man leaves a woman with a son, a sons behaviour may deteriorate or
he may step up to the big plate,
But when a man leaves a woman with a daughter,
It's like a man leaving a lamb,
In constant fear of the slaughter,

Men you need to realise that you sons are strong,
They may turn out just like you,
Or they may grow up and prove you wrong,

You need to realise your daughter will always have issues,
She will look for a father figure ,
Just because she's missed you,

If you walk away from the ex or your baby momma,
You need to go back and collect you child without the drama,
This isn't a stage you don't need to perform,
You need to be the one that remains mature,

Because I'm sure if you turn up with a calm persona,
Your ex can't ever be the girl who will try to own you,
She may be the one that will constantly phone ya,

But that's because she sees your reliability,
Taking care of your responsibilities,
Don't abandon your son because he'll grow to hate you,
Don't abandon your daughter because she'll always date you, in all of her
future relationships,
She'll never have a guide to avoid the shit,
And that's all your fault, you can't blame mommy for the end result,

If you aren't there to protect your child,
How do you expect another man to respect your child?

The Profit & The Poet

Introspective

I've watched ex's become lesbians,
Stupid people become thespians,
I'm never shocked or surprised when the snakes say let's be friends,

Nothing in life should be hard at all to figure,
Racists speak on statuses type the "N word",
Because they know deep inside its wrong to type N……,

But the irony is they are steeling,
Stealing history,
With no feeling,
And while the mass appeals
are appealing,
People still get boxed in by their ceiling,
Sealing their own fate when they start revealing,
Their true thoughts show a deeper meaning,

A lost way without asking for direction,
Is a loss due to introspection,
But on more examined inspection,
We just need an intervention,
By a stranger that usually gets rejection,
Because they come from a perceived enemies perception,

Shall I apologise for the N word,
It burns my soul to type the full verb,
But to communicate it clearly,
I believe in no fear so you can hear me,
And if you know me,
Then please show me,
Your true heart,
Not the show pony,
No time for tricks,

The Profit & The Poet

I'm no magician,
It's a miracle that's my mission,
To unite the racists with the race less,
To be recognised only by name,
Not the colour of faces,
Because I guarantee if you trade places,
You will all be following my footprints to set those paces,

To end this discrimination,
That's the hard part,
But look in to your heart,
That's where your journey will either fail or succeed,
That's the real start...

R.I.P Jermaine "GUS" Brown

**I miss you bro,
I still have you rapping on my phone you know,
All the times we spoke about you helping me with the shoes and clothes,
Now I can only hear your voice when I play your video,
God has finally taken you home.**

<u>Be the Change</u>

I wasn't put on this earth to make change,
I was put on this earth to be the change,
So while everybody talking away,
swalking a way,
I'm walking this way,
You see I Run
Dis Man Cum,
DM's C me I won't run,
I weigh a Ton,
But not Tun up,...
Late never,
I'm on time for the come up,
But wait,
what does all this mean?
Nothing if you aren't clever,
It's not even cryptic,
It's not balloon talk,
or helium,
My words are burners,
Like Josh's-sticks they smoke,
But I'm not concealing em',
I put em out here for everyone to see,
Because I'm like that,
I only hide behind me,
So I'm out here in the open,
I'm out hearing every word that gets spoken,
That doesn't make me a spoken word artist,
It makes me work hard,
Cuz when I work art,
It's like I cropped a farm,
And reaped the harvest,
I don't do substances unless it is substantial,
When I uplift,
The shift of power is financial,

The Profit & The Poet

Build a school of education, without the city council,
Because when I counsel,

The message is substantial,
In a big way where we create a trusted association,
No need for illegal activity in a basement,
Jacks about to blackout does Cassie know,
I think she's getting educated by this albino,
Asked many times in my life to pick a colour,
Tick a box to separate me from my brother,
Just another way to get us fighting one another,
But knowing what we have learned we just won't bother,

The tools they tried to tighten up our shackles,
Are the hooks that caught the fish without the tackle,
But as we read and see the truth inside the lie,
The more the True story lives and HIS-story dies,
Now I can just sit back and not say another word,
But if I get one like on Facebook,.
I am blessed somebody heard,
somebody read it, understood it and observed,
because one day these lines will not be blurred...

The Profit & The Poet

Higher Learning

You can do a thousand great deeds and not get recognised,

But do one bad deed and the world will destroy you even if you apologise,

We are gonna do wrong even if we think what we're doing is correct,

Poor choices, listening to the wrong voices in your head,

That doesn't make you evil,
And it doesn't make you bad,

And listening to those voices doesn't always mean you're mad,

It means you have a conscience that will guide you if you let it,

But we always make the wrong call when we're running out of credit,

Don't forget it,

Remember to learn the error of your ways and correct your life from those
mistakes,
It's called a higher consciousness when you repair your errors ,

And then your path and journey become straight,

It's not about their opinions as they also live like this day by day
But while they sit in judgement of you, they are being judged the very same
way,

If you are wiser from your past and your future's looking brighter,
You have learned your lessons well and you can see your dark clouds of
misfortune lift,

And your days will become brighter

<u>Stranger Part 2</u>

On her way home,
She always smiles
I wish she would pause,
Take a breath,
Sit on my step for a while,

Always in a rush,
Does she know she's my crush?
I don't ask her for change,
I just admire her immensely,
If we ever spoke,
Would she tempt me?

I bet I'd fumble my words
She really isn't like these other regular birds,
She is beautiful,
That smile does so much,
All I know about her,
Is she catches the 45 bus.

The Profit & The Poet

This journey

Its taking so long to find home,
I could take this short cut but miss out on the journey,

I wish I knew the purpose of life,
Everything I try to find my purpose,
Burns me,
I take the back seat sometimes but then it takes a lot longer to get off,
There are days when I have a plan but like a bomb with no detonator,
I don't set off,

I struggle to meet the criteria I need to complete this mission,
I don't even know some of my facts from my fiction,
A walking contradiction,
Every day I live I'm watching others progressing,.
I stay Faithful and loyal, but I never feel like I receive a blessing,

so I question?

My journey, is my path already planned out,
Is this the life that I thought would pan out,
I'm lost in a maze,
don't know whether it's just pea soup or a haze,

many ways to find home but how,
I don't even drink,
But I'm stumbling now,
Nothings black and white its grey and cloudy,

I feel trapped, imprisoned
But no walls around me,
Perceiving the world like I'm lost,
My journey so far has incurred a cost,
I've suffered loss, of focus of family of friends,

But still I see no journeys end

The Profit & The Poet

I'm wandering,
Pondering,
Am I lost or found,
Is this silence in my heart,
The real sound,

Vibrations cause my life to continue on,
My journey to find a place called home

The Profit & The Poet

Sex Miseducation

Imagine a staircase that only goes round,
Is it elevating yourself,
Even if you pressed down,

Sex educated in a council stairwells,
Wipe your chin with a mouthful of
Farewells,

School hasn't taught you, the streetz did that,
Thinning on top, ...
Butt getting fat,

It's a trap, it's a system,
Like a porthole,
You poor morsel ,
Nobody missed you while you miss them,

Also let's get off topic,
A take off your top pic,
Your just made a boob, you're a top tit,
Top tip, for a tip top,
Ice cold pole,
Is this still sex education
Or am I getting old,

Am I still addicted to this life
Readers wives,
I can't afford fiesta,
Found my dad's stash,
While he was having a siesta,

The Profit & The Poet

He wasn't awake to teach me any different,
Only time he was in,
He was inconsistent,
That's why I'm so different,
Teach my kids how to be persistent,

Ask questions on sex and I'll answer,
Because they want to learn; I need to know the answer,
I won't be nappying,
No time for pampers,
You are my babies but you still need an answer,

Sex education is a sore subject in the home,
But teenage pregnancies are caused in the home,
Parents shy away from every taboo,

Won't ever happen
Til it happens to you,

That's the ignorance of the uneducated,
Nine months with a bump,
Now the mums deflated,
no dad around, everyone saying
I told ya,
You'll manage luv,
You're a single mom soldier,.

Imagine a staircase that only goes round, is it elevating you,
And your buggy and your frown,
On your own in a high rise flat,
Your teenage daughters been pressed down from the back

In the same stairwells you had your fornication,
Do you understand the importance of the streetz truthful education,

The Profit & The Poet

It's a cycle like a hymen you can break it
One leaves a bloody mess,
I suggest option two
You should take it

Break the cycle,
Don't ride it,
You man are boys,
They will tell that you'll like it,
Ignore them, they will still call you slut,
Better to be the and or an if not a butt,

Don't be free with it, Cuz its gonna cost you,
That future job isn't gonna want you,
15 hours childcare that's all you get free,
Wait until you're educated,
Before you try for babies

Children having children,
Doesn't have to be the cycle,
What take the Richard?
Is it because if you don't,
They'll take the Michael??

Outreach

They offer so much but actually give me so little,
I am sure they get money from the man in the middle,
The funding they get,
Where is it all going?
They drive new company cars,
But they are not out here showing,
Us how to get off the streets,
And we have no way of knowing,
How to help ourselves,
If they just remain silent,
We raise our voice,
They call the police,
Saying we're aggressive and violent,
These are the people who are in a position to help.
But as they drive through that puddle in their shiny new car,
The message is clear,
They're only helping them self.

The Profit & The Poet

<u>Abandoned ship</u>

They've all abandoned ship
No one for companionship
Floor was wet, I guess they slipped,
With me there's No rush, no trip
Sorrow to see they had no grip
Hollow until I feel sick
Hollow until my clothes don't fit
Sorrow hoping it all ends quick
The smile is tension stiff
All because they've abandoned ship...
Tomorrow's a new day but right now that don't exist,
Wallowing?...that won't fix sh*t!
By your standards I'm not perfect...
I guess that's it,
I can run in circles, jump through hoops, leap hurdles & not get fit
& still they'd abandon ship,
In the dark, now only one candles lit,
Tumbleweeds are stationary,
they replace those who by me, use to sit,
In the loneliness of growing,
the gears get shift,
They've left the room & turned off light switch,
Solitude, "real-eyesation",
home gets hit,
When my cloth is torn, I fix with woven stitch
No hard feelings when they abandon ship,
Everyone's busy pushing & pulling Captaining their own ship,
But The lion's den victor's victorious in this Championship
& then The anchor lifts like I planned this sh*t.

(Dan Man 2014 ©)

The Profit & The Poet

The Stranger no more

She noticed me yesterday,
With her smile greeting my face,
Today she came back,
To my place,

Where I was sitting,
She asked why I kept staring,
And before I could answer,
Her boyfriend was swearing,

My illusion shattered,
I might even get battered
All those compliments
I paid her in my head,
None of that mattered

Now she is in my face,
Talking about reporting,
Me for stalking,
The misconceptions of my societal position,
Now I wish I'd begged instead,
At least she wouldn't have looked today,
And just kept walking

I put all my trust in a stranger,
Daydreaming of our first meeting,
Has left me in danger,
Now I just hope she can control
Her disgruntled fiancés
Anger

The Profit & The Poet

Trust

Who can I turn to apart from this needle?
The outreach don't reach out,
They won't come out to my spot,
Scared I think of the mess and upheaval
I wish I could soar like an eagle,
And look down from above,
I wander if up there in the air,
There is any more love,
Does God exist would my plight be clearer to him?
When I look up from here,
I see my life flash by as the pin,
Pierces my skin,
And I realise if I go now,
I better pray,
I will be nearer to him
I don't trust my dealer,
I don't trust myself,
I don't trust the police either,
I don't trust the Centre's,
They tell me are there to help
There is only that one Geezer,
He comes out at night,
A follower of Christ,
He doesn't just bombard me with food,
He sits and he listens to my story,
He got these wicked Nikes for me,
He really is doing something good

Do I trust him, I'm not sure?
But his heart seems' pure
They call Him Streetz or the Preacher.

What is Father Deficit? By Craig Pinkney and Dr Sangeeta Soni

Many people ask what father deficit is. This is particularly an important question for those working with young people.

Father deficit centres on the psychological impact on individuals whose fathers are not present, which leads to an unfulfilled need. This need concerns the lack of a father figure consistently present in the life of an individual, especially someone who is young, and therefore in the process of growing up. When this need is not addressed or confronted, can often lead those affected to seek solace in deviant groups, susceptible to violence, substance/alcohol misuse, depression, anger, etc. By belonging to such groups a young person effected by father deficit may seek out 'alternative' figures or transfer the impact of father deficit into other behaviour.

Females are impacted in the same way as males but manage it differently. Essentially the most important man in your life is absent, and then the impact can be devastating at key points in your life.

Healing, grieving, acknowledging the pain and repairing the gap left by this loss is part of a long-term solution.

Healing

Father deficit does not just refer to the idea that an individual does not have a father present in one's life, for example perhaps because of a splitting of parental relationships, imprisonment or death; rather it can also be due to a father being present but it may be one who has no emotional or physical connection to their child. For example, a father who works doing multiple jobs or works in a demanding job and as a result rarely has time to spend with his

children. Such a father may try and compensate for his absence by giving his child/children gifts or money.

The Profit & The Poet

The concept of the potential damage caused to a child by the loss or absence of a caregiver is not a new one because for many years now social psychologists have focused on the concept of attachment and the impact of broken attachments (for example through the work of Bowlby or Rutter). Therefore, the idea of the impact on a child or young person who does not have a caregiver in their life has a long history.   However, the focus specifically on the effects of a lack of a father in one's life is only now beginning to be researched in more depth.

We live in a society now where not only the father has to work but also mothers often do so too, just to keep the balance or perhaps because they are single parents. Therefore, the possible impact of an absent father, when a mother too may be busy working and therefore have limited time and attention for a child/children may further compound the situation. Moreover, you have other mitigating factors resulting in dysfunctional families with external factors such as substance misuse, poverty, reconstituted family structures etc. often playing a part amongst many other possible factors.

Males generally demonstrate signs of difficulty during adolescence, a period when the young male is trying to shape and define his masculinity. If there is not a positive and consistent male role model in his life, then often such a young man may find that he shapes himself by drawing on a range of distorted ideas of what masculinity is. In the process of doing so, such a young man may seek out other, perhaps less ideal role models. This could be anything from a celebrity, entertainer, sports star, local musician or prominent members of criminal groups. Through these distorted notions of masculinity, some develop something which is called hyper-masculinity, which in essence is an exaggerated form of masculinity where behaviors and actions are over exaggerated, particularly in regard to ideas relating to what it means to be 'a man' in society.

This in many cases may therefore mean that young men effected by father deficit may be violent, aggressive, abusive, intolerant, often the result of the impact of a lack of a father figure on their emotions, but it also may be based on behavior that may be modelled by their chosen role models.

Father deficit can also have a positive impact on men and women as due to this experience of not having a father or male present in one's life, many try their best to break that cycle so that their own children do not have to go through the same situation as they did. They have an understanding or empathy with what it means to have an absence of a father in one's life and therefore use the experience to create a different future for their own children. However, not every person who has experienced father deficit can use it for such a positive purpose. For many it becomes a source of frustration, anger and hurt that becomes expressed in many more negative ways.

The Profit & The Poet

Thanks and acknowledgements

Firstly, I have to thank God Almighty and Christ (when I first started writing at 9 years of age I used to wander why everyone thanked God and not their mom and dad) for guiding me to the point in my life where I finally feel that I can Be a Voice for the people that I have had the pleasure to learn so much from.

So My thanks go out to the homeless Community in Birmingham, particularly the following two men, Patrick "Paddy "Morris and Stuart "Griff" Griffiths who looked after me and taught me so much in our time together. It is with Gratitude that I mention these two amazing people who are both no longer sleeping rough, at the time of writing, Griff is engaged to be married.

Paddy you hold a special place in my heart, from showing me how to make a cardboard mattress to the time you treated me to a free coffee at McDonalds with your vouchers.

I give thanks to my Parents, although we do not always get on, I owe you a whole lot, you gave me life. Say no more.

To the Community of Birmingham, To the Artists I know, the entrepreneurs, the wise Brothers and sisters who bought me in to their Circle, to my Face Book Followers, who shared my statuses when I asked and even when I didn't. To the other poets and scholars who have contributed to this book, all I can say is Wow. Thanks is not a powerful enough word.

To filmmakers who always tried to get me on camera to say something, to my City, this is for you.

Just a few of the many people who have encouraged or sat and shared with me, who helped the Give Back Project or just literally showed me love:

Meeks, Dan-man, Juice Aleem, Ben Ryan, King Cipher Jewelz, Malik MD7, Felicity (Tash), Simeon (Zim), Tobeijah (Rev), Adam (OD), Mike (Shuts), Marv(MDR), Brasko, Carl Morgan, Natasha Benjamin (dad), Marcus Distant, Natalie King, Sic'nis, Justice Williams, Robin Thompson (Rev Assassin), Dr Martin Glynn, the entire Royalist Family, Shutdown family,

The Profit & The Poet

YT, DaTwinz, The Miccoli Family(Buy their album),Quartz Crystallus, Earl Douglas, Alan "Fingy" Thompson, Celia, Julia (Lozells Church), Shareen, Sonia, Gary, J'neil, Nanny Alfred Road, Waseem Zaffar, Elijah Phillipps,10th Planet, Marc (Cutsodeep), Cipha Divine, Sarah Richards , Soella, Seyi, Maria, Henry, Annika, The Creatives, One Mile Away, Mark Barnett, Invasion, Vader, Sox, Lil Choppa, GL360, R.O.P.P. Daniel Anderson, Daniel Alexander, Diggy,Bamz, Curtis, Bossman, Deniro, DfollowmeZezi, Zezi, Queen Kadi, Doreen, Birmingham is ours. #brumtown #Givebackbrum

To Sharon "Shazza" Thompson thank you for taking the Fight to another level. We on this sis.

Martin, my photographer, but more than that, my friend, who inspires me in life. Your work is amazing. Thank you my brother.

Nathan" SKIPPA" Dennis, Brother your heart is your grace, your love is God's glory. You're a true inspiration.

D, your story from then until now is an inspiration for all of us. Growth is imminent, Truth is your legacy.

Last but by no means least.
My three children, you are my world, my sole inspiration to show you the world through my eyes, so that you have a head-start on all your rivals, my eldest son Zachary, from the fun and wrestling to the back shaving and beard shaping. Son I love you xx.

To Daniel my Superhero, the boy who is way ahead of your time, the boy who hits hardest and hugs tighter than anyone else. Son I love you. My superhero xx.

To Erykah, if only you knew what you mean to me. Oh wait, I can tell you here, you are the most amazing woman I know, had the pleasure to speak with and listen to, the smartest little girl and yet the wisest lady, nobody will ever hold you back. I am sorry we don't always get on. I Love you Ery xx.

Streetz Preacher. The Give Back Project